This Easter book is presented to

....

by

....

on

....

THE   EASTER   CAVE

The Easter Cave

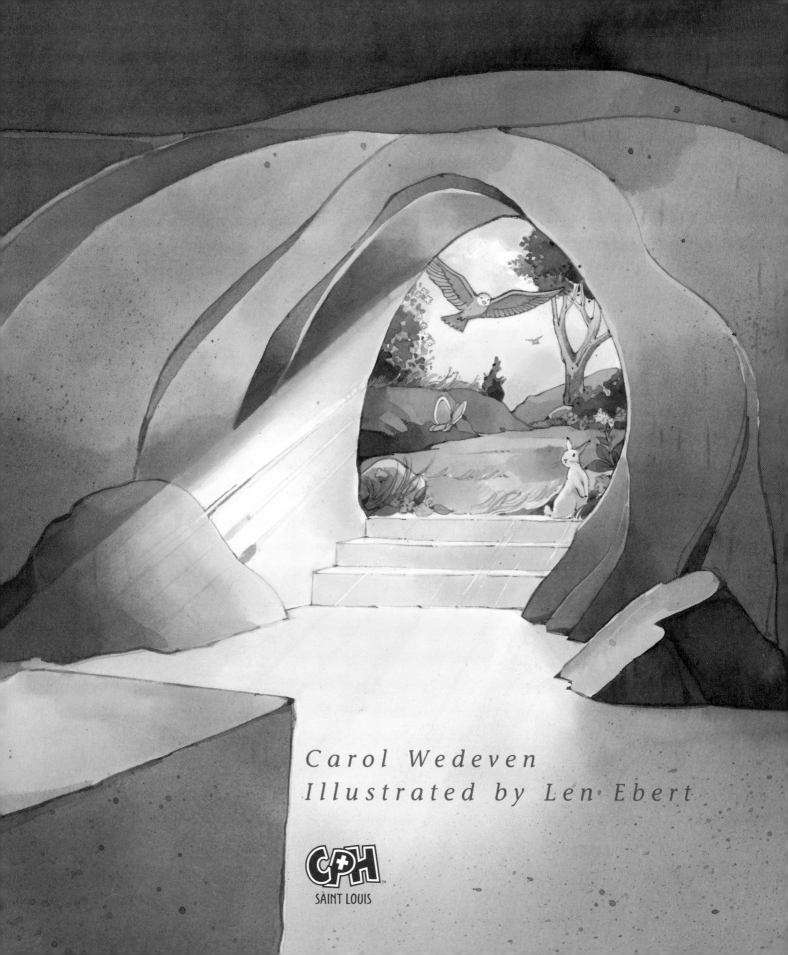

Carol Wedeven
Illustrated by Len Ebert

CPH
SAINT LOUIS

As evening approached,

there came a rich man from Arimathea,

named Joseph ...

[who] took [Jesus'] body,

wrapped it in a clean linen cloth,

and placed it in his own new tomb

that he had cut out of the rock.

He rolled a big stone in front of the

entrance to the tomb and went away.

(Matthew 27:57–60)

This is the cave the friend gave.

This is the bird

That crowed near the cave the friend gave.

This is the King

That heard the bird

That crowed near the cave the friend gave.

This is the crown

That scratched the King

That heard the bird

That crowed near the cave the friend gave.

These are the men

That made the crown

That scratched the King

That heard the bird

That crowed near the cave the friend gave.

This is the cross with nails that sting

That stood near the men

That made the crown

That scratched the King

That heard the bird

That crowed near the cave the friend gave.

These are the women who cried that spring,

That watched the cross with nails that sting

That stood near the men

That made the crown

That scratched the King

That heard the bird

That crowed near the cave the friend gave.

This is the stone, a giant thing,

That puzzled the women who cried that spring,

That watched the cross with nails that sting

That stood near the men

That made the crown

That scratched the King

That heard the bird

That crowed near the cave the friend gave.

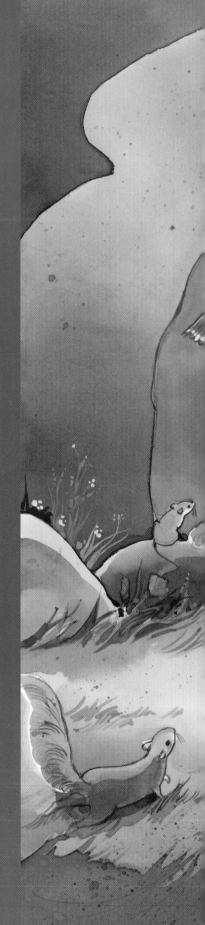

This is the angel on shining wing

That rolled the stone, a giant thing,

That puzzled the women who cried that spring,

That watched the cross with nails that sting

That stood near the men

That made the crown

That scratched the King

That heard the bird

That crowed near the cave the friend gave.

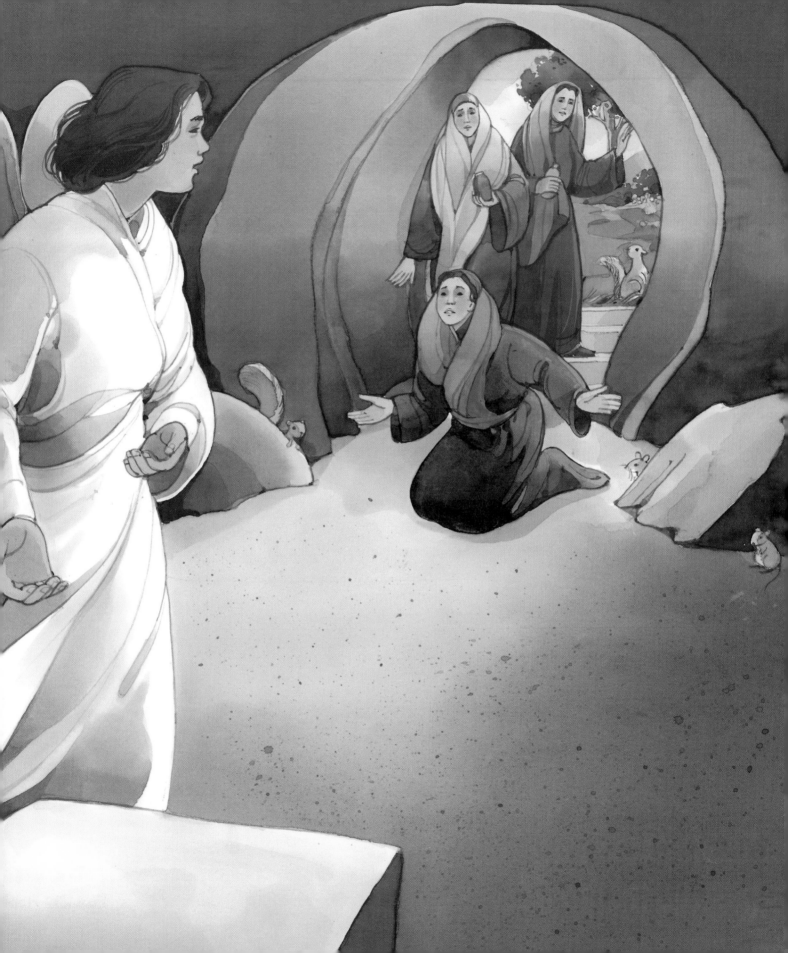

These are the friends with good news to bring

That heard the angel on shining wing

That rolled the stone, a giant thing,

That puzzled the women who cried that spring,

That watched the cross with nails that sting

That stood near the men

That made the crown

That scratched the King

That heard the bird

That crowed near the cave the friend gave.

He is not here; He has risen!

(Luke 24:6)

This book is dedicated to

Liesl, Rachel, Graham and Christina;

Mike, Aaron, Chellie and Jeff—

more of God's gifts blessing me daily.

T H E   E A S T E R   C A V E

Scripture quotations taken from the HOLY BIBLE, NEW INTERNATIONAL VERSION®. NIV®.

Copyright © 1973, 1978, 1984 by International Bible Society.

Used by permission of Zondervan Publishing House. All rights reserved.

Text copyright © 2001 Carol Wedeven

Illustrations copyright © 2001 Concordia Publishing House

Published by Concordia Publishing House, 3558 S. Jefferson Avenue, St. Louis, MO 63118-3968

Manufactured in the United States of America

.		3	4	5	6	7	8	9	10
10	09	08	07	06	05	04	03	02	01